MW00439142

Lecaz, Dorian Jacquez
  French Swear Words: A Systematic Guide to Fluent French Swearing. – 1st ed.
  ISBN: 1451567995   EAN-13: 9781451567991
            Book design by Maestro Phrasebooks.
          Printed in the United States of America

French Swear Words

A Systematic Guide to Fluent French Swearing

By Dorian Jacques Lecaz

Table of Contents

-1-

Introduction

Why most French swearing books don't work and this one does.

Open up your average slang dictionary. It doesn't matter if it's French, American or Russian. What is the main problem there? Well, if you buy most American slang book targeted at Russians you will notice that they seem to be quite extensive. However, usually 80% of the terms included in those slang books are, well, worthless, out of use, or do not give appropriate details on usage.

And imagine how weird a foreign speaker would sound when trying to use all these out of date, regional and other obscure slang expressions when speaking English? It will be funny, but unintentionally.

So, what does all of this have to do with swearing in French? Dissatisfied with availability of quality material and systems that teach how to swear in French, I decided to develop my own.

This book gets right to the heart of swearing. I will quickly go through the basic and essential vocabulary for French swearing, slang, and euphemisms.

For the most part, French has not changed that much over the past century. Because French is a language limited by the strict rules of the Academy, both the proper language and the slang are significantly more limited than other languages, such as Russian, where stringing together colorful swear words is, in fact, an art. Whereas the words and slang of English seem to undergo constant cultural changes, French is kept under strict lock and key and, in fact, has significantly fewer words than the English language! Rough estimates put French at 35,000 words while English has 170,000 words.

In other French-influenced countries around the world, however, this rule is less true: French Quebecoise is littered with many English words, offensive and otherwise, throughout the language. Arabic and Carribean countries also have more colorful slang leftover from their original cultures.

Nevertheless, this, too, is beginning to change as the world becomes more and more globalized and other cultures begin to influence the French language -- specifically English and Arabic. While watching French MTV, you'll hear the English word "booty" frequently used. You'll also hear "kif-kif," a word borrowed from Arabic meaning "the same" (C'est kif-kif / It's the same).

Verlan: Verlan is a kind of French pig-latin, used most often by French youth, but there are a few words that almost everyone in Paris will be using that I will cover in this book. To understand the Verlan, reverse the first and last syllables or letters of a word. "Eu" is also often added to the middle of the word, but this is not always true, as you will see from some examples. Although you can virtually say any French word in the Verlan, I will cover a few of the basics-- and a few of the most offensive!

Students of French and foreigners often come into the country with great French skills, but without the knowledge of how to use the casually, resulting in an overly-refined sounding speech. There are a few tips I can offer to overcoming this dilemma:

1. When forming a negative verb (for instance, Je n'ai pas / I don't have), drop the "ne" before the verb. "Je n'ai pas" will transform into a more conversationally and informal "J'ai pas" to use with friends and family. However, you should continue to use it for business, writing, and any other more-formal situation.

2.) Often pronouns and verbs will be joined to form a single word in conversation. For instance, instead of saying "tu as vu le film?" you would say "t'as vu le film?"

Lastly, we will not try to make up for lack of organization or systematic thought with humor. Instead, we will use an organized, precise system that will enable you to swear using words that are actually used. For every mentioned examples be sure to construct three of your own; this should be plenty of practice.

Although I don't condone the use of derogatory words, especially those aimed at underrepresented populations, it is, however, important to be aware of what those words are in order to move fluently and fluidly in another language. Because I believe that the dissemination of knowledge cannot be limited to values or politics, I am including words in this book that I sincerely hope you will *never* utter. Instead, my hope is that by learning these words (specifically those related, for instance, to homosexuality), that you will be an informed citizen and speaker of the French language, knowing and yet above the hatred that some of these words carry.

Others, however, are much less serious and much less political. Words such as "putain," "merde" and "foutre" are exceptional ways to litter your conversations with curse words. Use as liberally as you please!

-2-

Fundamentals of Swearing

In French

The main words you need to know to swear effectively in French.

French swearing is not terribly different from American swearing as far as the intent of it goes. So, what are the reasons you may want to learn swearing in French, just like in English?

First of all, swearing is used for emphasis. For example, the phrase "What the fuck was that?" is not different from meaning of "What was that?" The main difference is the emphasis that makes the phrase stronger, more poignant and expresses your strong or aggressive feelings about the issue in a more powerful way.

Secondly, swearing is used for personal attacks. For example: "You dirty fucking bastard" is much more powerful than "You not very good person." People frown down on swearing but it really does express a form and feeling, which cannot be expressed in any other way. Thus, in this way swearing can be very apt and powerful.

Lastly, swearing is often used for talking dirty or to enhance our sexual experiences.

French swearing is not different in this regard. In this chapter we will introduce the basis of French swearing that will then be applied to two main areas: Emphasis and Personal Attacks. The coming chapters will explore some other relevant words.

So, without further ado, here are the basic swear words that the French use on an everyday basis.

<u>Primary Swear Words</u>
Baiser – To fuck

Enculer – To fuck

Foutre – To fuck

Niquer- To fuck

Une Salope – Slut

Un Putain – Bitch, whore

Une Connasse – Cunt

Un Con- Asshole

As you may have noted, "fuck" comes in many varieties in French. In fact, to be all inclusive, you could also add "coucher avec" as a translation for "to fuck," although it hardly merits as cursing; the translation is more consistent with "to sleep with" and is not considered offensive.

In order to say "fuck" appropriately in French, then, one must know which words are most appropriate in which situations.

As a general rule, "coucher avec," "foutre," and "baiser" are more sexual and less offensive variations on the word while "enculer" and "niquer" are more offensive and insulting. "Niquer" is most commonly used in immigrant communities, although its use is becoming more and more pervasive among the natives as well.

Moreover, because "fuck" is such an environmentally-dependent word, as opposed to the way in which the word functions as a noun, adjective, verb, or exclamation in English, in later chapters we will cover further varieties of its use in speech and grammar.

"Foutre" is a verb meaning "to fuck" or, more precisely "to cum." Foutre is generally less in use than other words for "fuck," but is still seen in other, derivitative curses, such as "va te faire foutre!", meaning "go fuck yourself!", or "son fou," which means "whatever" and is not considered offensive. It should be noted that this word is very close to and often confused with "foudre" which means "lightning."

The word "salope" is generally used to refer to someone as slutty, but can also translate as a pejorative for "prostitute." "Putain" is a fairly commonly used word. Conversationally, it is also often used the way one might use "shit." For instance, one could say:

J'ai essayé conduire ma voiture ce matin et, putain, elle c'est cassée!

I tried to drive my car this morning and, shit, it's broken!

Note that "putain" doesn't translate literally to "dammit", but its function in this sentence has the same effect.

Honorable Mentions
Enculé – Bastard
Merde – Shit

Putain (functionally)– Shit

Une Vache – A Cow

Connerie – Bullshit

Chier – To Shit

Pisser – To Piss

"Shit" is not as offensive as some of the words in the primary category and is used frequently by both adults and children. In a sense, it can be translated merely as "rubbish." "Piss" is also not an offensive word and is used in a lot of different situations.

Although calling someone a cow in English is mildly insulting, it is far more common and far more offensive in French, on par with calling a woman a slut. Use it carefully! The word can also be used as an adjective to call something nasty or disgusting.

Example 1: Cette femme est trop vachement.
Translation: That woman is too disgusting / sloppy (literal translation: cowly).
Example 2: Je veux pas tes pieds vaches sur moi!
Translation: I don't want your nasty feet on me!

Une Bite – A Dick

Des Blobos- Fat, Droopy Boobs

Une Chatte – A Pussy

Un Cul – An Ass

Une Clito – A Clitoris

Des Cuilles – Balls

Un Gode – A Dildo

Un Oignon – An Asshole (Literal translation: an onion)

Un Presrvatif – A Condom

Enculer – Anal Sex

Mouiller – To Get Wet

Se Branler – To Masturbate, To Jerk Off

Sucer – To Suck

Lecher – To Lick

Note: If you'd like to tell someone to jerk off, "Va te faire foutre!" is more appropriate. Remember that "se branler" is reflexive, so it will take the following to form agreement with pronouns:

I jerked off / Je me branle

You jerked off / tu te branles

He/she jerked off / il/elle se branle

We jerked off / nous nous branlons

They jerked off / ils/elles vous branlez

Grammar

Baiser or to fuck is conjugated in the following way.

Present tense:

I fuck / je baise

You fuck / tu baises

He/she fucks / il/elle baise

We fuck / nous baisons

They fuck / ils/elles baisent

Past Tense:

I fucked / j'ai baisé

You fucked / tu as baisé

He/she fucked / il/elle a baisé

We fucked / nous avons baisé

14

They fucked / ils/elles ont baisé

<u>Imperfective Past Tense:</u>

I fucked / je baisais

You fucked / tu baisais

He/she fucked / il/elle baisait

We fucked / nous basions

They fucked / ils/elles basaient

-3-

Swearing for Emphasis

Put more punch into your French phrases.

The following is a list of words that are used for emphasis solely to show strong feelings, anger, disgust, amusement, surprise or just about any other strong emotion. Now let's do a series of case studies to get a feel of how these work.

De merde – Fucking (as an intensifier)

Here is how this word is used for emphasis in French: Adding "de merde" converts fuck into an adjective. Then, same as in English, you can attach this adjective to just about anything to demonstrate your strong feelings about it. Note that "de merde" as an adjective is most often used about inanimate things, usually when something is not up to your standard. So, this part is the same as English. But in English, you can say, for example, "I fucking told you to do it." Can't use it like that. Also, when you say de merde about something in French it's always negative. So you can't say "That's fucking awesome" in French, as calling something "de merde" always gives it a negative connotation. So keep that in mind. Here are some typical examples of how it's used.

Example 1: L'ordinateur de merde marche pas.
Translation: The fucking computer doesn't work.

17

Example 2: L'ecole de merde est fermé aujourd'hui à la neige.

Translation: The fucking school is closed today because of the snow.

Example 3: Mon prof de merde m'a raté.

Translation: My fucking professor failed me.

Merdeaux – Shitty. Derived from "merde," you can use this as an adjective.

Example 1: C'est merdeaux.

Translation: That's shitty.

Putain. Just like in English, sometimes you can just say putain for emphasis. That can be used to indicate just about any emotion. It can be positive or negative. Usually though, it includes elements of amazement and surprise.Although "putain" doesn't translate to "fuck" directly, its functional use for emphasis is the same.

Example 1: Putain! Il y a beaucoup de biere!

Translation: Fuck, there's a lot of beer!

Example 2: Putain! Quelle fille! (Demonstrates amazement.)

Translation: Fuck! What a girl!

Example: Putain! J'ai rien des cigarettes Demonstrates disappointment.

Translation: Fuck! I ran out of cigarettes

De bordel. This word is used in nearly the same was as "de merde" and is interchangeable. It can be used to add emphasis or to say something is shitty.

Example 1: J'essaye regarder la télé de bordel!

Translation: I'm trying to watch the fucking television!

Example 2: C'est bordelique.

Translation: That's shitty.

Putain – Bitch Stick it at the end, beginning or middle of just about any sentence and it adds emphasis.

Surprise or disappointment. "Putain" can function easily as a method of expressing exclamation of any sort.

Example 1: Putain! Où sont-ils?

Translation: Shit! Where are they?

Example 2: Quand j'etais defonsé, j'avais marché à la rue et, putain, j'ai vu mon prof!

Translation: When I was drunk, I was walking along the road and, shit! I saw my teacher!

Example 3: Le magasin est fermé? Putain!

Translation: Store is closed? Shit!

2. Anger. Often during a confrontation, "putain" is used to taunt the offender.

Example 1: Où est l'argent, putain?

Translation: Where's my money, bitch?

Example 2: Porquoi tu parles à ma copine comme ça, putain?

Translation: Why are you talking to my girl like that, bitch?

Connard / Connasse / Con – Asshole, Bastard, Bitch, Cunt.

The "con" family of curses in French are fairly flexible. The form of the word is dependent on the gender of the subject: "Connard" is used for men or for masculine agreement. "Connasse" is used for women or for feminine agreement. "Con" is more neutral and can be appropriate for a wide range of subjects. "Con" is a markedly more offensive words than many other French swear words and should be used in caution-- only use it if you want to offend someone!

Example 1: J'ai entendu dire que t'es une connasse.

Translation: I heard that you're a bitch.

Example 2: Ouais? J'ai entendu dire que t'as une petite bite, con.

Translation: Yeah? I heard you have a small dick, asshole.

Believe it or not, that's it. These are the main phrases used to express emphasis in French. Because of the way in which the sheer quantity of words used in French are fewer than other languages, such as English, many words will instead have ambiguous or multiple functions. "Putain," for instance, can be used in a variety of situations and remain appropriate.

Nevertheless, these simple words, used as adjectives and intesifiers, can change the emphasis of your words. As we progress throughout the chapters, we will further discuss the ways in which you can use these words and their other, situation-specific derivatives.

-4-

Blending Swearwords for Emphasis

Blend them to magnify the effect.

We've done this a bit before but let's practice this more so you can gain a better understanding of exactly how this works.

Again, the three main words we have are: putain, de merde, de bordel.

Let's take any regular sentence and practice infusing it with emphasis through all these great swear words we've learned.

Example 1: T'as pas vu ce film?
Translation: You haven't seen this film?
Example 1 + Swearing: T'as pas vu ce film de merde?
Translation: You haven't seen this fucking film?

Example 2: Je vais acheter des bieres.
Translation: I'm going to get some beer.
Example 2 + Swearing: Putain! Je vais acheter des bieres de merde.
Translation: Shit! I'm going to get some fucking beer.

Example 3: Où est mon chapeau?
Translation: Where's my hat?

Example 3 + Swearing: Putain, Où est mon chapeau de bordel? Merde!

Translation: Bitch, where's my fucking hat? Fuck!

Example 4: Mon équippe a raté hier.

Translation: My team lost yesterday.

Example 4 + Swearing: Putain, mon équippe de merde a raté bordelique hier! Merde!

Translation: Fuck, my fucking team fucking lost yesterday! Shit!

Example 5: Quelle type de fromage est ceci? C'est cher.

Translation: What type of cheese is this? It's expensive.

Example 5 + Swearing: Putain, quelle type de fromage de bordel est ceci, connasse? C'est cher de merde!

Translation: Fuck, what kind of fucking cheese is this, bitch? It's fucking expensive!

Example 6: Où est mes chaussures?

Translation: Where are my shoes?

Example 6 + Swearing: Où est mes chaussures des merdes, putain?

Translation: Where are my fucking shoes, bitch?

Lastly, a more famous string of swear words strung together was uttered in *The Matrix Reloaded* by the beloved Frenchman: "Putain de bordel de merde!" This string of curse words signifies no real semantic meaning other than utter frustration.

-5-

Personal Attacks

Tell them all you think about them.

Personal attacks are the other main reason most people use swear words in any language and French is no different. Thus, let's outline the main words that can be used to insult someone.

Connard/Connasse/Con: The "con" words are popular in French and can be translated as "bastard," "asshole," "bitch," "jerk," or "cunt." For men or for masculine agreement, use "connard." For women or feminine agreement, use "connasse." "Con" is also another version of the masculine insult.

Example 1: Mon prof est un connard.

Translation: My teacher is an asshole.

Example 2: Ma copine me parle pas parce qu'elle est une connasse.

Translation: My girlfriend won't talk to me because she's a bitch.

Example 3: T'as volé mon vélo, con!

Translation: You stole my bike, jerk!

Un Pauvre Con – A Dumbass, A Fuck-up

Braleur / Branleuse – Idiot. This is only a mildly offensive word and can be used for either a male (-leur) or female (-leuse). It is often used to refer to someone as rather insignificant.
Example 1: Il est un branleur de merde.
Translation: He's a fucking idiot.

Example 2: Porquoi est-ce qu'e la branleuse ici?

Translation: Why is that idiot here?

Salope – Slut. This insult is quite common to refer to a woman as a slut or whore.

Example 1: Ta copine est une salope.

Translation: Your girlfriend is a slut.

Salop / Salaud – Bastard. The male compliment to "salope," "salop" generally means "bastard," "jerk," or "asshole."

Example 1: Ton copin est un salop.

Translation: Your boyfriend is a jerk.

Enculé – Bastard / Asshole. This insult is derived from the word "enculer," or "to fuck."

Example 1: T'es un enculé!

Translation: You're an asshole!

Enfoiré – Bastard / Asshole. Used in the same way as above.

Example 1: T'es un enfoiré!

Translation: You're a bastard!

Pute – Whore. Derivative of "putain," "pute" has recently come into speech.

Example 1: Pourquoi t'as volé ma chemise, pute?

Translation: Why did you steal my shirt, whore?

Un Pousse-Crotte – A Push-Shit. This is an extremely offensive word used to refer to homosexuals.

Une Meuf – A Woman. "Une meuf" isn't actually insulting at all, but a part of Verlan: re-arranging the "f" and the "m" from "femme" and adding the "eu" creates the word that is often used on the street.

Example 1: T'as vu cette meuf?

Translation: Did you see that woman?

Un Mec – A Guy. Complimentary to the "une meuf" Verlan, although it remains a mystery as to how "mec" is derived from "homme."

Example 1: Je voudrais coucher avec ce mec.

Translation: I would like to sleep with that guy.

Un Keuf – A Cop. Verlan for "cop." Probably not wise, however, to say this to an actual cop.

Une Teuf – A Party. Verlan for "party".
Example 1: Tu vais aller à la teuf?
Translation: Are you going to the party?

Un Gros Gaule – An Ugly mug. A swear word that refers to someone's face as beast or animal-like.
Example 1: Ferme ton gros gaule!
Translation: Shut your ugly mug!

Va chier – Fuck off (literally: go shit).
Example 1: Je veux pas te voir. Va chier!
Translation: I don't want to see you. Fuck off!

Nique ta mere – Fuck your mother. This insult functions identical to the way that you would say it to someone in English. While "niquer" is often use, "enculer" is also appropriate here.
Example 1: Va niquer ta mère!
Translation: Go fuck your mother!
Example 2: J'ai niqué ta mère hier soir.

Translatoin: I fucked your mother last night.

Example 3: : J'ai enculé ta mère hier soir.

Translation: I fucked your mother last night.

Fils de pute – Son of a bitch. Same as English, although "pute" refers to "whore" more than "bitch." "Pute" is also a derivative of "putain."

Va te faire foutre – Fuck off. Probably the most common French insult, this is the equivalent to the English "fuck you".

Va te faire enculer – Fuck off. Same as above. "Foutre" is used more commonly, but both "foutre" and "enculer" are used as translations for "fuck" as insults in French.

Un Trou du Cul – An Asshole. This literally translates to the same English insult and is used in the same way-- meaning that it is equally offensive, as well!

-6-

Swearing for Everyday Things

When a regular word just doesn't cut it.

Swearing is not used just for emphasis or insults. Sometimes swear words happen to express the meaning of everyday things and are used as such.

This doesn't mean they don't add emphasis or are free from offensive meaning. Actually, they are quite full of both of these things. Regardless, these words are out there and if you want to be an advanced French speaker and don't want to be left out of any conversations there will be invaluable.

Péter – To Fart. For this verb, the accent changes to a grave when conjugated. You should also be careful with this verb because of its phonetic similarity to "répeter," "to repeat". If said without the accent, the unwitting foreigner actually says "repeter," or "fart again."

Example 1: Ce vieil mec pète.

Translation: That old guy is farting.

Péter plus haut que [son] cul – To fart higher than one's asshole. This is similar to the way in which English speakers note the way in which a snob's shit must smell like roses when they're clearly too full of themselves.

Je m'en fous – I don't give a fuck.

Example 1: Je m'en fous de lui.

Translation: I don't give a fuck about him.

J'ai rien à foutre – I don't give a fuck.

Example 1: J'ai rien à foutre avec lui.

Translation: I don't give a fuck about him.

Laisse be'ton / Laisser Tomber – Let it go. This literally translate to "to let to fall."

Example 1: Je veux pas le parler. Laisser tomber.

Translation: I don't want to talk about it. Let it go.

Mal de – To get sick of.

Example 1: J'en ai mal de merde de ce prof.

Translation: I am fucking sick of this teacher.

Example 2: J'en ai mal de cette chanson de merde.

Translation: I'm fucking sick of this song.

Qu'est-ce que tu fous? – What the fuck are you doing?

Example 1: Putain! Qu'est-ce que tu fous?

Translation: Shit! What the fuck are you doing?

Niqué – Fucked. Use "niqué" in the adjective form to refer to something as "fucked" or "broken."

Example 1: Ma voiture est niqué

Translation: My car is fucked (broken).

Example 2: Hier soir était niqué!

Translation: Last night was fucked!

Les Mensonges – Lies

Example 1: Je le crois pas. Il dit des mensonges.

Translation: I don't believe him. He tells lies.

Example 2: J'en ai mal des mensonges de merdes!

Translation: I'm sick of listening to your fucking lies!

Menter – To lie.

Example 1: Pourquoi est-ce qu'elle m'a menti de bordel?

Translation: Why did she fucking lie to me?

Example 2: Il ment toujours.

Translation: He always lies.

Piquer – To steal. "Voler" is the formal word for "to steal" whereas "piquer" is slightly more informal, to be used with friends and family.

Example 1: Qui a piqué le feu?

Translation: Who stole the lighter?

Example 2: Il pique le vin du magasin.

Translation: He steals the wine from the store.

Foutu – Fuck / Fucking. "Foutu" is yet another word for "fuck," derived from "foutre." Add this as an adjective or adverb to your conversations for emphasis.

Example 1: Qu'est-ce que tu en as foutu?

Translation: What the fuck did you do with that?

Example 2: Où est-ce que je l'ai foutu?

Translation: Where did I fucking put that thing?

Merde – Nonsense or sucks.

Example 1: C'est merde.

Translation: That's shit.

Example 2: Ce film est merde!

Translation: This film is shit!

Son fou – Whatever.

Example 1: Où est-il? Son fou!

Translation: Where is he? Whatever!

Example 2: J'ai raté l'examen. Son fou.

Translation: I failed the exam. I don't care.

-7-

Euphemisms

When you want to soften the effect.

French, just like English, has quite a series of euphemisms, which are usually phrases that sound close to their swearword counterparts, but yet without the extreme offensive meaning. The phrases and words below are derived from their offensive counter parts but can be used with less caution.

Une Pipe – A Blowjob. Probably one of the most famous French euphemisms. Take a look at Magritte's painting "Ceci n'est pas une pipe" and perhaps you'll have a different interpretation this time!

Example 1: Elle m'a fait une pipe.

Translation: She gave me a blowjob.

S'en battre (les couilles) - I don't care / I don't give a shit.

Literally, this translates to "to beat the testicles."

Example 1: Il l'a piqué. S'en battre less couilles.

Translation: He stole it. He doesn't give a shit.

Un Chauve à col roulé– An Uncircumsized Penis. Literally: the bald one with the turtleneck. There are a fair number of uncircumsized men which has led to the popularity of this phrase.

Example 1: J'aime son bitte. Il a un chauve à col roulé.

Translation: I like his dick. He's uncircumsized.

Un Cigare – A Dick. Literally: a cigar. This euphemism is mostly commonly used as "fumer un cigare," to give a blow job" where "fumer" literally means "to smoke."

Example 1: Tu veux fumer un cigare?

Translation: You want to smoke a cigar? / You want to give me a blowjob?

Une Cramouille – A Wet Slit. Generally used if someone wants to refer to female genitalia in an unpelasant way.

Example 1: J'ai conduit un autobus par sa cramouille

Translation: I drove a bus through her wet slit.

Enlève ta croute que je swingue dans l'pus – Take your scab out, I'll fuck in the puss. This is an extremely vulgar utterance, generally used merely for shock value or comic effect for how absurdly offensive it is.

Une Moule – Vulva. Frenchmen compare the lips of the vulva to open mussels, which is what the word literally translates to.

Example 1: J'adore ta petite moule.

Translation: I adore your little mussel.

Un Poulet – A Cop. Literally: a chicken. As with most slang dealing with cops, would be wise not to use this word to their faces.

Example 1: Ce poulet m'a vu piquer les biers!

Translation: That cop saw me steal the beers!

Un Queue – A Prick, Dick. Literal meaning: a tail.

Example 1: Où est ce queue?

Translation: Where is this dick?

Ramoner – To Fuck. Literally, this means "to sweep the chimeny," which is compared of the in-and-out motion of intercourse.

Example 1: Nous avons ramoné toute la nuit.

Translation: We fucked al night.

Service Trois Pièces – Three Piece Combo. This is a phrase used to refer to the two testicles and shaft of the penis, generally when referring to a blowjob. "Service" in this sense is playing off diner-talk, as one would refer to coffee with cream and sugar.

Example 1: Ah ouais, je veux le service trois pièces, s'il te plaît.

Translation: (Sarcastically) Ah yeah, I'd like the three piece combo, please.

Tirer – To Pull or Shoot. Euphemism for ejaculating.

Example 1: Je vais tirer!

Translation: I'm going to shoot!

Une Zigounette – A Dick.

Example 1: J'adore ta petite zigounette.

Translation: (Insultingly) I adore your little dick.

Une Souris – A Mouse/A Small Girl. Euphemistically, this is used to refer to a small or younger girl as an object of desire.

Example 1: Je te jure cette pettie souris me veut.

Translation: I swear to you that little mouse wants me.

Une Verge – A Twig/A Small Dick.

Example 1: Son fou. T'as une verge.

Translation: I don't care. You have a small dick.

Zinzin – **Crazy.** This word has no real meaning other than its colloquial use for "crazy" as an adjective.

Example: Il est trop zinzin, tu vois?

Translation: He's too crazy, you know?

-8-

Index of Words/Phrases

Baiser – to fuck

Bite – (f) dick

Blobos – (m) fat, droopy boobs

Branler – to masturbate, to jerk off

Branleur / Branleuse – Idiot

Chatte – (f) pussy

Chier – to shit

Cigar – (m) blowjob

Clito – (f) clitoris

Con -- (m) ass

Connasse -- (f) bitch, cunt

Connard -- (m) ass, bastard, jerk

Connerie – (f) bullshit

Coucher avec – to sleep with

Cuilles – (f) balls

Cul – (m) ass (relating to the body, not insulting necessarily on its own)

Cramouille – (f) wet slit

Enculé – bastard

Enculer -- to fuck in the ass

Enfoiré – bastard / asshole

Fils de pute – son of a bitch

Foutre – to fuck, to cum

Foutu – fuck / fucking

Gaule – (m) face

Gode – (m) dildo

Keuf – (m) cop

Lecher – to lick

Mec – (m) man

Menter – to lie

Mensonge – (m) lie

Merde – (f) shit

Merdeaux – shitty

Meuf – (f) woman

Mouiller – to get wet

Moule – (f) vulva

Niquer – to fuck

Oignon – (m) onion; asshole

Pédé – (f) faggot

Péter – to fart

Pipe – (f) blowjob

Piquer – to steal

Pisser – to piss

Poulet – (m) chicken; cop

Preservatif – (m) condom

Putain – shit, fuck, slut

Pute – (f) whore

Ramoner – to fuck

Queue – (m) prick, dick

Salope – (f) slut

Salaud – (m) bastard

Service Trois Pièces – three piece combo

Souris – mouse; small attractive girl

Sucer – to suck

Teuf – (m) party

Tirer – to shoot; to ejaculate

Vache – (f) cow

Verge – (f) twig; small dick

Zigounette – (f) dick

Zinzin – crazy

39585836R00032

Made in the USA
Middletown, DE
19 January 2017